LIVING MEMO

of Merseyside

The late 40s, 50s and early 60s

A photographic journey
around the Liverpool area
from the camera of ***Keith Medley,***
selected by ***Steve Barnes.***
Captions by ***Colin Hunt & Cliff Hayes***

PP

PRINTWISE PUBLICATIONS LIMITED

47 Bradshaw Road, Tottington, Bury, Lancs BL8 3PW.

Warehouse and Orders:
40-42 Willan Industrial Estate, Vere Street, Salford M5 2GR
Tel: 061-745 9168. Fax. 061-737 1755.

Book organised, everybody chased and badgered, tunnel fees paid by and a round of drinks bought by

Cliff Hayes

ISBN No: 1 872226 19 1

All the photographs in this book — and many others — are available for your home, business or office. Copies can be obtained from Steve Barnes at

LIVING MEMORIES,

Westbourne House, 96 Westbourne Road,
Oxton, The Wirral,
Merseyside L43 4TQ

Telephone 051-653 3536 (24 hr.)

Printed and bound by Manchester Free Press, Paragon Mill, Jersey Street, Manchester M4 6FP. Tel: 061-236 8822.

FOREWORD

It's often been a complaint of mine that all today's nostalgic photo books are "before my time". I want to see photos that I can associate with, photos to bring back memories, photos that I can shout "Oh yes! I remember that".

Being born in 1942 my childhood was really from the late 40s to early 60s (I was a slow developer) and at last here are the photographs I've always wanted. Photographs of the city centre, crammed with people and trams. Windows with prices like 19/11d, £2.4s.6d etc. Advertisements for Atlas Bulbs, Mothers Pride, Bev. Shops we thought we had forgotten. Sterling Shoes, Hope Bros., Hyams, Times Furnishings, Herbert Wolf jewellers.

But the photographs of New Brighton, are the gems. The outdoor fair, the Tower grounds, the Swimming Pool, they are all here. Photographs that bring back an innocence of youth I thought I had long forgotten, the days when going "over the water" was the nearest you ever thought that you would get to the continent.

If you're lucky there could be an additional bonus for you in this book. "YOURSELF". Are you the boy in white pumps pointing out to sea; are you one of the three little ones on the donkeys. Is that you (when you had a good figure) splashing about in the pool; is that you dancing at the Tower or the Grafton, may be that is even your mother with the milkman.

Enjoy these pictures and let them bring back the priceless pleasure of memories.

Billy Butler

Steve Barnes

As a collector of photographic memorabilia I must have spent many hundreds of hours during recent years sifting and sorting through old photographs, postcards and prints, usually a few at a time, looking at scenes that no one alive today could possibly remember. When, during the summer of 1991 I was given the opportunity to select and print from the Keith Medley collection, there was only one possible title that we could give it. Living Memories...

Here, before my very eyes, was a photographic lifetime built of over 300,000 glass plate negatives professionally taken during the 1940s, 50s and 60s that would offer almost everyone an identifiable view of their past. We hajve only just begun to explore this glass encyclopaedia that offers us images of everything from fashion to furniture throughout our region during three exciting decades.

Acknowledgements

To those friends, without whose help this book would never have existed, I include, Claire Ashley, for her photographic expertise, Joy Hockey, for saving, storing and sorting the negatives, which might have been thrown away!, and Vince Clegg and Robert Owen for the loan of some of the collection from my Studio in Wallasey, which they now operate, as Creative Photography, I tender my grateful thanks. **Keith G. Medley**

The publishers would like to express their thanks to Colin Hunt for being so helpful with the captions and showing his immense knowledge of times and dates of the pictures and Paul Brookes for his hard work on the book.

Potted History of Keith G. Medley

Keith served his photographic apprenticeship in Liverpool — one of his first jobs took him to the top of St. George's Hall, taking pictures of the opening of the first Mersey Tunnel.

Then he headed for London and a job with an advertising agency covering the Lever products. He spent the next few years photographing cakes, puddings and food — all cooked in the nearby kitchens — Spry and Trex, as well as other products like Lifebuoy soap, which featured beautiful girls in bubble baths.

A chance meeting with Howard Coster found him working in the great man's Studio as an assistant and meeting such people as A.A. Milne and his small son Christopher Robin, Leon Goosens, Aldous Huxley, and other famous writers who came into the Studio.

When War broke out, he returned to Liverpool to wed Eileen Deakin, at Crosby Registry Office, and soon afterwards, was called up and posted to the Marine Aircraft Experimental Establishment in Scotland, filming the first Bouncing Bomb experiments in Sunderland Flying Boats. Then on to the photographing of parachute drops of jeeps, guns and commando troops, Poles and Free French as well as our own Troops, and parachute drops of supplies for the Maquis.

On being demobbed after the War he came to Wallasey to open a Studio with a colleague, Bob Bird, covering local weddings, studio portraits and press work for local and national newspapers, and in 1960 added news reel filming for Movietone News and Granada T.V. News. He was at Coniston when the Donald Campbell saga took place and Campbell lost his life attempting the water speed record; the Investiture of Prince Charles at Caernarvon, and the funeral of Sir Winston Churchill in London.

His studio was moved from King Street, to Liscard in 1984 where he took part in the Charming Child competition for the Wallasey News, and says that he must have photographed most of the children in the town as babies. He retired in 1987, and left the studio to younger men, settling down to a quieter life, reading, doing crosswords and trying to make friends with a very superior cat which has adopted him.

October 1991.

THIS BOOK BELONGS TO

____

(insert your Co-op Divi Number Here ____________________ *)*

How serene and civilised Church Street looks. Liverpool cleans up after the war damage and the bomb sites get cleared and ready to re-build on.

Buses and Trams together along Lord Street. Hope Brothers, the shop that launched a thousand school uniforms lies on one corner. Horne's on the other corner has yet to be built.

ST George's Crescent, Lime St at night showing The Imperial Hotel, The Washington, The V. P. sign and the Guinness Clock all now long gone and sadly missed. Replaced by a load of anytown Pre-cast Blocks.

It's a bit more difficult crossing the road here now-a-days.
The junction of Moor Lane and Liverpool Road, Crosby.

Picton Clock and the High Street in the Mid-fifties. Someone should tell that driver he's going the wrong way round the island.

Jerome's in London Road where *EVERYONE* had their picture taken.

Sunday Morning window shopping in Bold Street. How uncluttered the pavements and roads (no yellow lines no posts with parking restrictions etc).

Ranelagh Street — looking up to the "Big House", when we had a real Central Station.

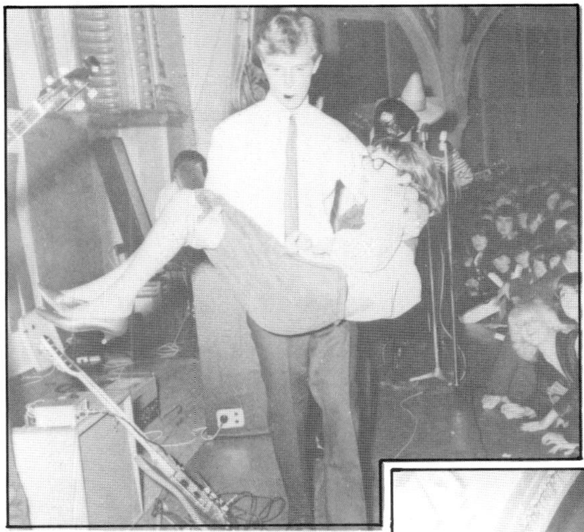

Stoned out of their minds. It was all too much for some fans when the Rolling Stones visited the Tower in Aug. 1964.

They're not ghosts in the corner it was sponsored by Rael Brook Toplin shirts.

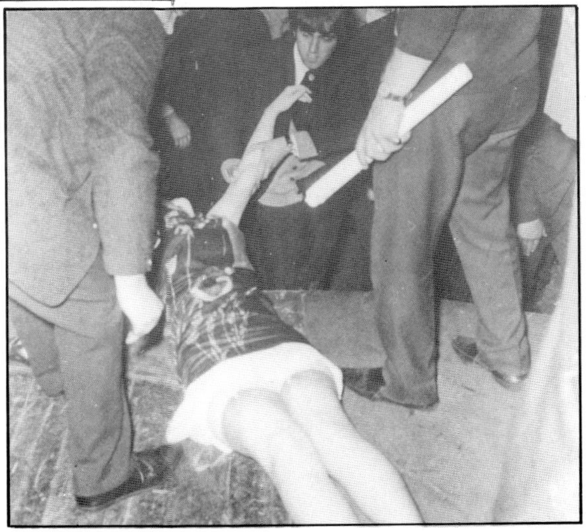

I bet no-one owns up to this picture. Were you at the Stones concert and recognise the dress?

"This is the B.B.C., Broadcasting from the heart of Liverpool, and now Monica Winstanley will read some knitting patterns. Sedate local radio at its vibrant best.

Looks like Billy and Wally to me.

Tales of the South China Sea, New York bars and Rio women to tell. Home port at last, with the smell of salt air in the nostrils and a view of the river.
But is it enough to quell the restless spirit?
The Mariner's Home Wallasey.

First in the queue — waiting for the baths to open.

I wouldn't say the old feller was mean, but this is the only picture of him pushing the boat out!

In the day when Benidorm was still a fishing village and foreign holidays were the preserve of the rich, you could still find the sun on your own doorstep. *Note the gondola baskets.*

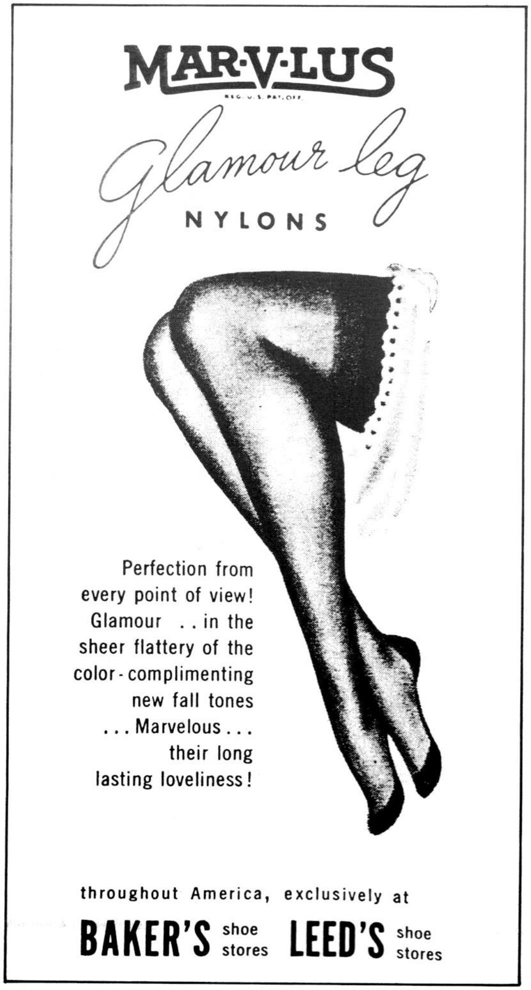

If you didn't have a car or couldn't afford to go to North Wales you could always get the train to West Kirby.

The Great thing about sea-side piers is that there's always somewhere to shelter when it rains.

I wonder what these five daring young ladies had done to look so pleased with themselves, perhaps you know one of the confident faces.

Once upon a time the ferries were so busy, you had to queue to get off.

V 24—10,000—5-37. [W. & S. Ltd.] (3769 G.C.)

London & North Eastern Railway.

TO

YORK

His weakness gives him **STRENGTH**

YES, the children have a very decided weakness for "Ovaltine" Rusks. Gratify this weakness, mother, for "Ovaltine" Rusks are a splendid strength-giver, especially if a cup of delicious "Ovaltine" Tonic Food Beverage is taken with them.

"Ovaltine" Rusks are made of wheaten flour combined with "Ovaltine." Highly nutritious, crisp, appetising and easy to digest, "Ovaltine" Rusks are delightful whether eaten dry or spread with butter or jam.

"Ovaltine" Rusks are of great value to infants when teething. They encourage mastication, which is necessary to ensure sound teeth and freedom from dental troubles in after-years. They are welcomed by invalids and convalescents, and are also most acceptable for family use in place of bread, toast or biscuits. Delicious in the form of a pudding.

'OVALTINE' Rusks

APPETISING DIGESTIVE & NOURISHING

Sold by all Chemists in 1/6 & 2/6 tins.

Remember Cherryade?

Anyone for tennis?

George Felton the donkey man at New Brighton in 1950.

A Metro Golden Scouse version of 'Baywatch'. Our David Hasselhoff look-alike (left) models the latest wooly swim wear, guaranteed to sag when waterlogged — and rub your thighs raw.

A cool Easter day in 1964 and people were out and about determined to enjoy the break, note the magnificent tower buildings, once the base of 621 ft tower which were to be burned to the ground 5 years later in April 1969.

A real grocers shop — heavy with the smell of cheese, coffee and bread and in the background the sinister whirring of the bacon slicer.

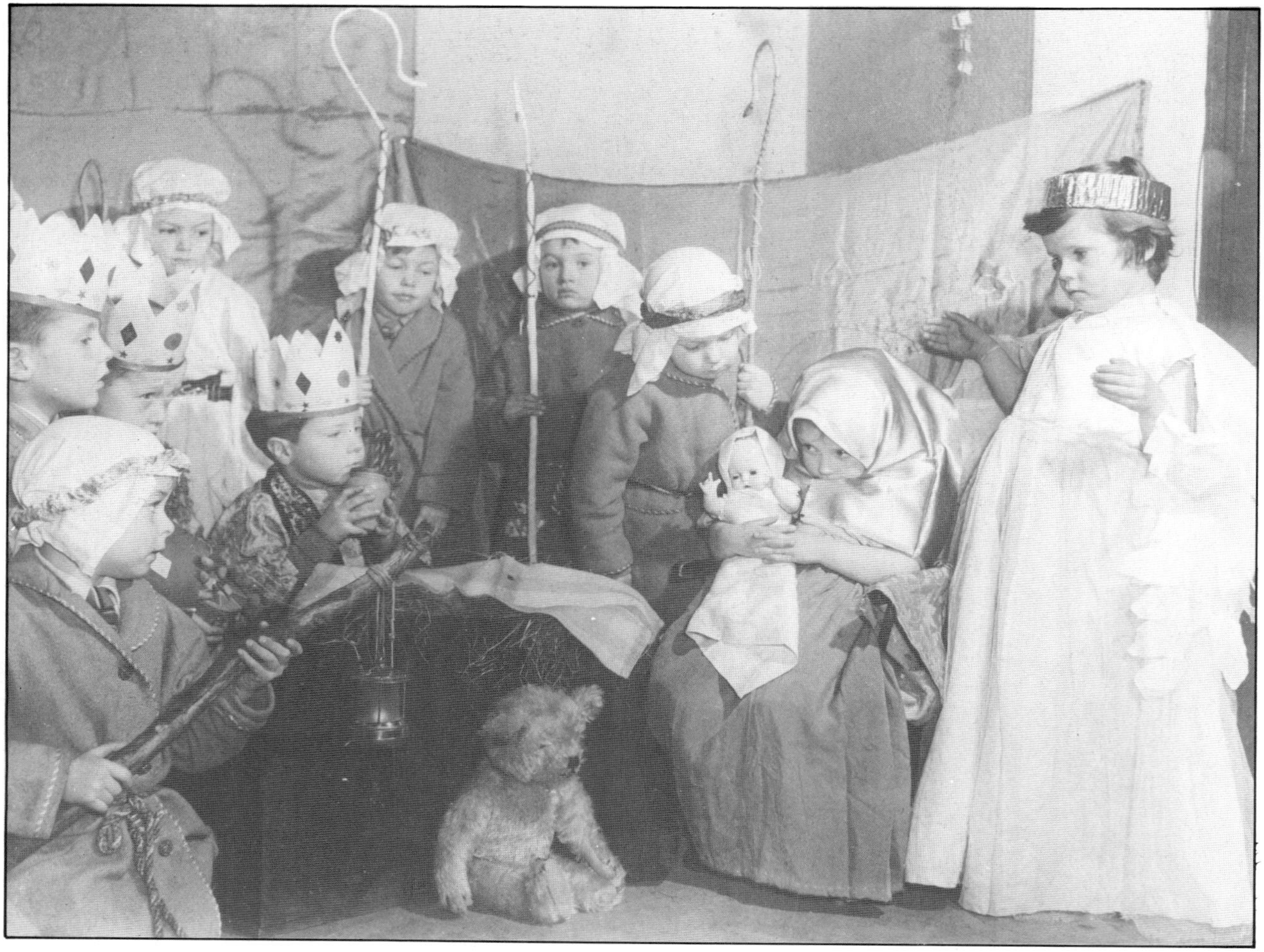

It's amazing how those shepherds 2,000 years ago all wore dressing gowns.

Lines Bros.
Famous Toys

Like an enchanted castle the illuminated pier at New Brighton floats above the dark waters of the Mersey.

The scorched hull of the Empress of Canada following the disastrous fire on January 25th 1953. Probably one carelessly discarded cigarette end did this to a mighty White Empress.

Lifting the Canada in Gladstone Dock March 1954.

2/- (Two Bob) for a grotto parcel in the days when your Christmas stocking contained a clockwork mouse, an orange, a bar of chocolate and some lead soldiers for the fort you never got.

In Spite of the march of 'H' aerials appearing on everybody's roof, village life still goes on in some areas. Eastham village on the Wirral.

Long shadows and an even longer pier. Is that the sea in the distance? Autumn light at Southport just after WW2.

How many people have struggled on a bus carrying one of these to a party. The ever present Dansette record player. No party or youth club hop was complete without one of these red or blue music machines.

Some things never change. Sunday mornings and a fleet of ice cream vans prepare to unleash their chimes on your neighbourhood.

Doreen, I told you not to give Mavis that second sherry.

The serene beauty of the ‘new’ Empress of Canada about to make her maiden voyage from Liverpool to Montreal in April 1961. The third ship to carry that famous name she was the last of the line of ‘White Empresses’ she left the Mersey for the last time on December 14th 1971.

Dock architecture at its finest. The distinctive clock tower at Nelson Dock, backed by the grandeur of the Stanley Dock tobacco warehouse.

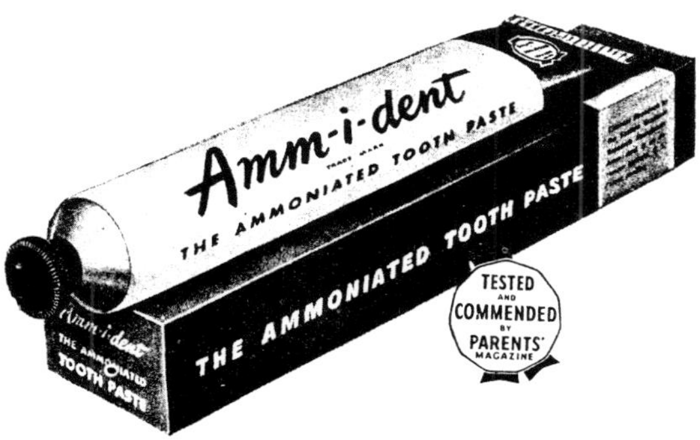

Vale Park in the days when the Cunarders went by within hailing distance.

A Stormy day on the river in September 1957. The Royal Iris battles her way to the landing stage which a high tide has risen to the level of the Pier Head. In the foreground a pair of Green Goddesses' shuttle to and fro on the 6A, the last route for Liverpool's trams.

A few years after the previous picture and the bus take-over is nearly complete. The Crosvilles at the front of the picture are off to exotic locations like Cronton and Rainhill Stoops.

Ship Spotting or just watch the Mersey go by, you can't fail to be impressed by the 'British Argosy. At 107,729 tons she was the largest ship to enter the Mersey when she headed for the Rock Ferry Terminal in the sixties.

As proud as if he was captain of the QE2, The Chief Officer of Mammoth, the Mersey's 200-ton capacity floating crane. Mammoth flexed its mighty muscles on the river between 1920 and 1986.

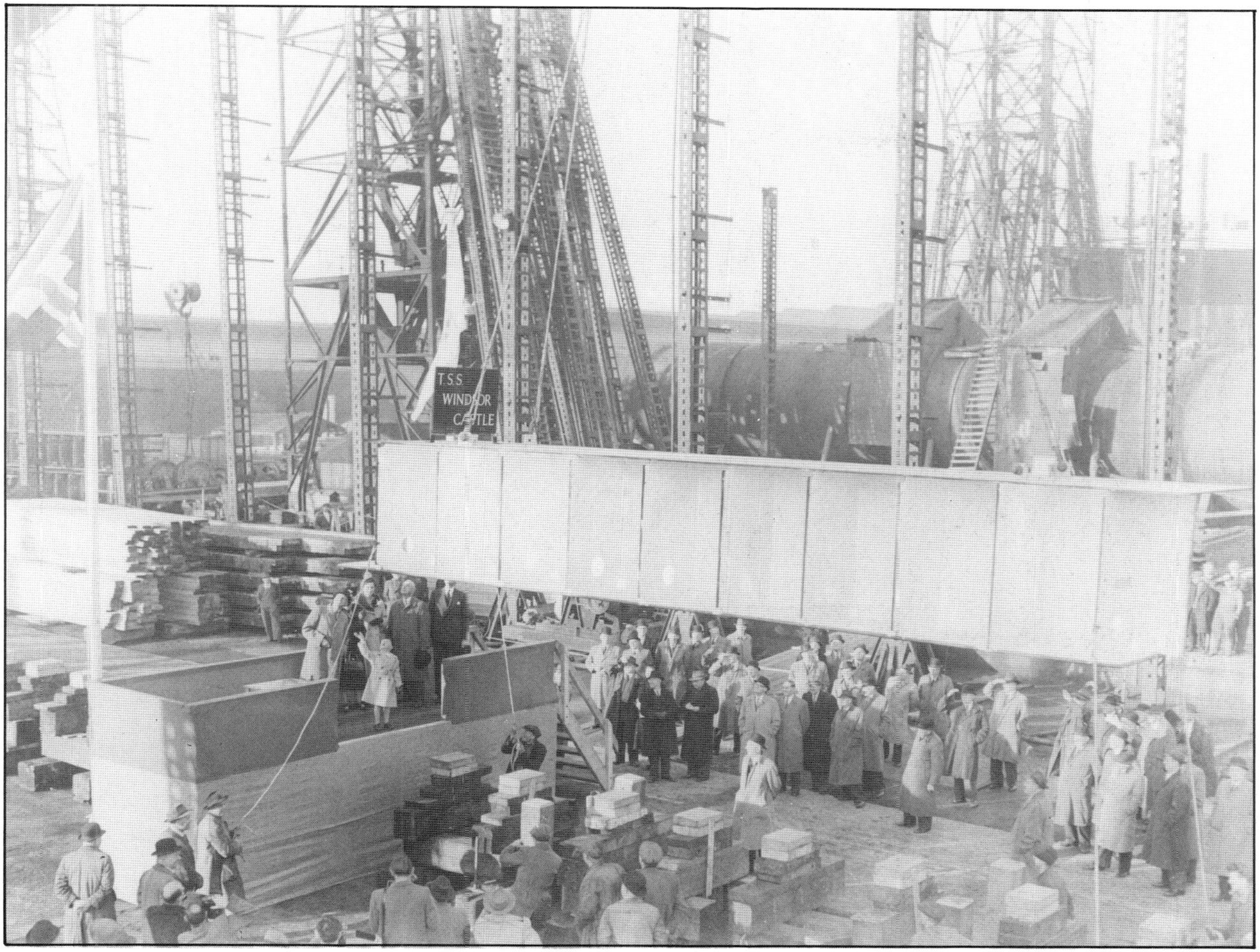

Following in the wake of the 'Mauretania', two Ark Royals and countless other vessels great and small, another keel is laid at Cammell Laird's. This one is the Windsor Castle.

Slow, Slow, Slow, Slow, Slow. Dancers frozen in time on the Royal Iris dance floor.

"I have to tell you anything you say may be recorded and used against you." High-tech policing, fifties style.

Summer queues for the tunnel down St. John's Lane. The kids in the sidecar in the centre of the picture must be suffering from Carbon Monoxide poisoning. A Morris van has pulled to the corner of Old Haymarket while the lads stock up with 'Bentox' for the day ahead.

Before the Clean Air Act of 1956 this was a common site, or it would have been if you could see it! It's another of those impenetrable 1950 fogs that stopped the trams.

"Morning Ken"
"Morning Nobby"! You look pleased with yourself" "I should say so! I've just met the new one at number 68".

"A free pint for me"
"Take it with my compliments. By the way, I'm a friend of Nobby's."

Love is . . . Evening Sunlight over the Marine Lake,
Southport.

Eccleston Ferry on the Dee. A great place for a picnic, complete with a cup of milky coffee with that distinctive 'Thermos' flavour.

It's no fun when you and your kid are the only ones at Sefton Park without a model yacht.

They're Off! In the 40's and 50's the Liverpool Marathon started on St. George's Plateau and finished at Anfield after the Reds practice match.

Excitement is high and the crowd threaten to invade the pitch as the winner breasts the tape at the end of another Liverpool Marathon at Anfield.

High School Confidential.

"Yes I know the pay's poor in nursing, but don't worry, it will improve in the future."

Ernest Marples M.P. signs up another Young Conservative.

"I don't mind the singing, its' the part where I have to kiss her I can't stand."

Now we know the secret of Hercules' strength, Mackeson!
"It Looks good, tastes good and by golly it does you good."

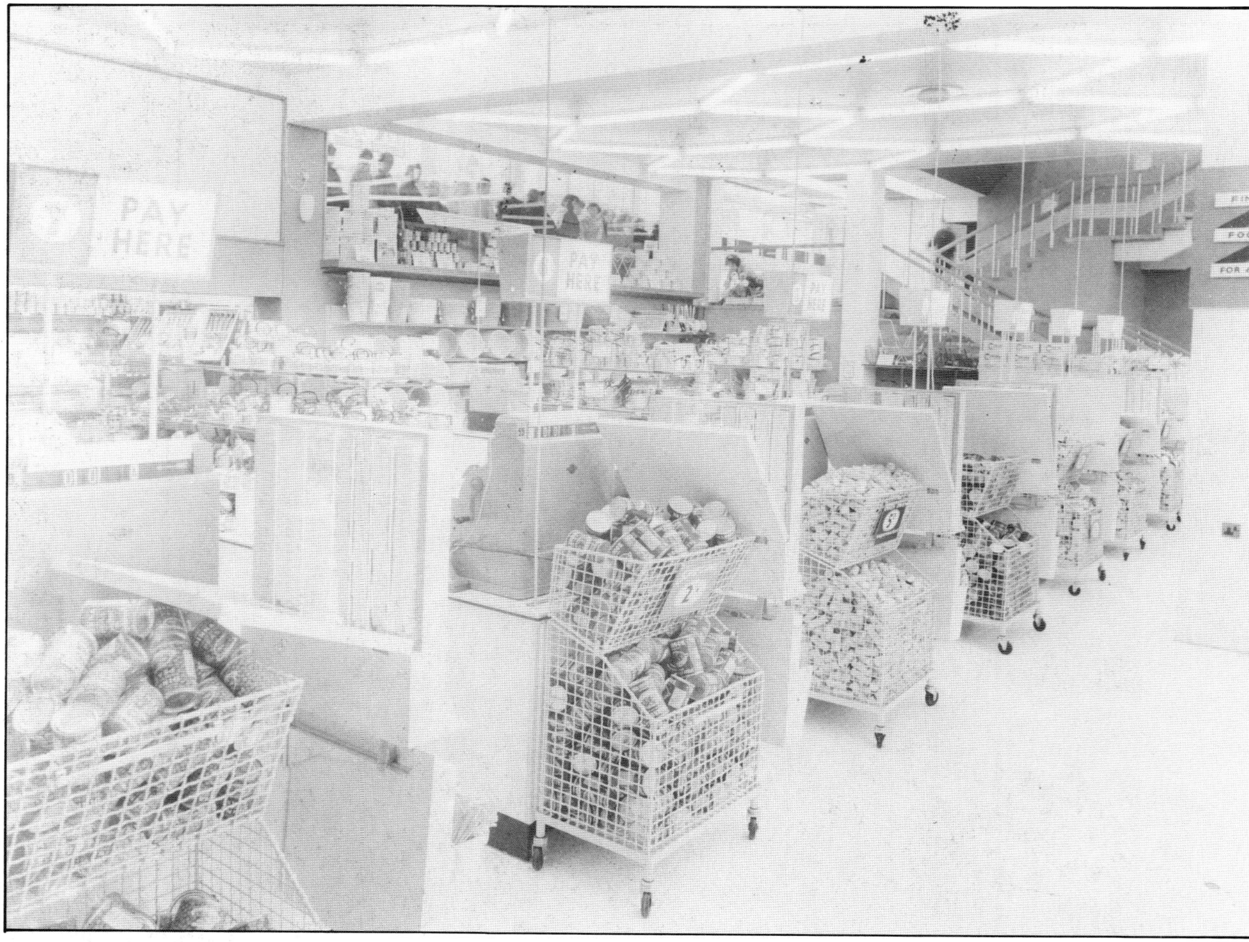

Check out the shoppers waiting to sample the delights of the new fangled supermarket.

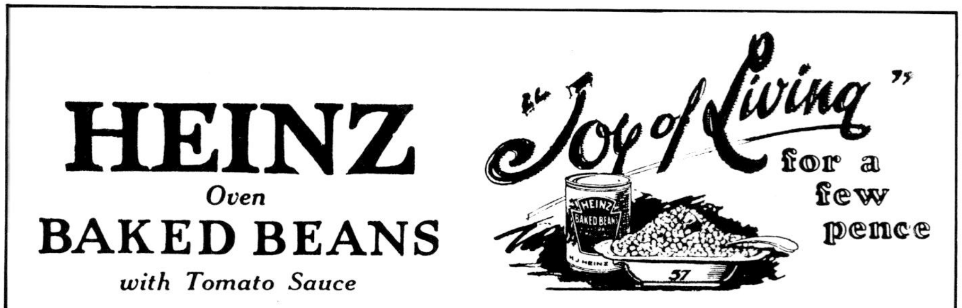

A slice of the country near the heart of the city.

Crosby village and order boys' bikes waiting for the lads to arrive.

Sunshine and shade from the "Docker's Umbrella'

Saturday Afternoon shopping in Whitby Road,
Ellesmere Port.

They don't build Show Houses like this anymore!

New homes for old. A modern prefab with all mod cons.

Even if you didn't back the Grand National winner you could join in the celebration at your local club or pub.

The brave new world of technology — The world's first regular hovercraft service ran between Leasowe and Rhyl in July 1962. The shape of things to come, or just so much hot air.

No, it's not a 1950 Minster for Decorating issuing free wallpaper to paper over the cracks in the post-war economy. It's giving out torches for the 1951 Festival of Britain Torchlight parade.

". . . and he told us of his life, in the land of submarines."
Underwater Christmas trees in town for the Festival of Britain.

The 1951 Festival of Britain was designed to uplift the nations spirits after the dark day's of war. More than ¼ million people watched the River Mersey pageant and Firework display on June 26th.

Like a giant candle Wellington oversees the Festival of Britain celebrations.

A "Mock Accident" gives Merseyside Civil defence an outing for their bandages. Realistic for the time.

In the fifties the docks boomed again, but change was on the way for "The Case Ball" "The Baldy Rabbit" "The Jelly" and the rest of the boys on the docks.

The Case Ball — Always getting laced.

The Baldy Rabbit — Lend us a tanner I've lost me fare

The Jelly — A bit of overtime and I'm set and and hundreds more.

Cast Iron, Steel Girders, the smell of Wet Timber
and one of the World's Great skylines
make this a picture of sheer artistry.

What is a small order for a place that size. 2 bottles of Sterrie and a crate of the milk of human kindness. These days you can get potatoes, bread, eggs, bread and even, some days, milk from the milkman. You can also get a nice cup of coffee and a meal from the Cathedral cafe.

Bucket and Spade at the ready.
All we want now is the sand.

One day he may be able to afford a real Fender, in the meantime he settles for a pair of Hank Marvin glasses and a guitar that looks like the real thing.

'Waiting for the crisps'. Another great Threllies fun night. We really knew how to enjoy ourselves in the 50's.

The old timers remember the Charleston, but for the young at heart there's always the Frankie Laine impression. Pity Karaoke hasn't been invented yet.

I'm getting Married in the Morning Ding Dong my head is going to hurt.

In olden days a glimpse of stocking was looked on as something shockin' but . . . In the late fifties High Street war-time rationing seems a million light years away in fact rationing on clothes only ended on March 15th 1949.

11 o'clock it'll soon be time for Worker's' Playtime.

I don't care if your name is Morris Cowley! You can't park there.

Happy Days! Happy Birthday 1957. But the great adventure still lies ahead, to be a teenager in the sixties.

After all these years of practising with Twink and Armani in the bathroom you can graduate to the real thing!

Nearly there! The span of the new road bridge is nearly complete, signalling the end of the Transporter bridge in the background.

The Britannic, last of the Great Liverpool liners, and last of the 'White Star' ships. She arrived home in Liverpool after her final Atlantic Crossing on December 4th 1960. She's pictured here in January 1961 leaving Liverpool for the breaker's yard. The legendary bull and blue and black colours stiffening in the chill Mersey breeze as she heads for the bar the last time.

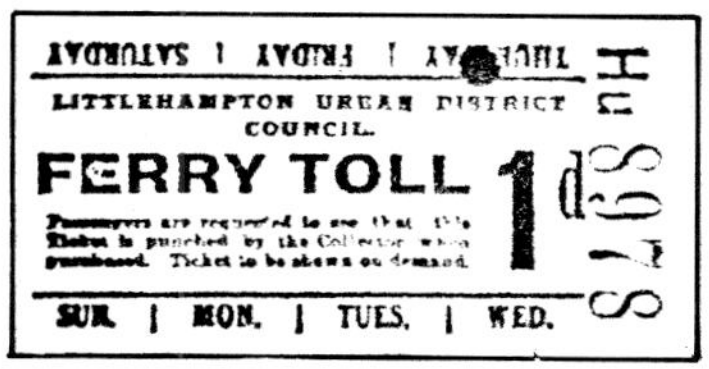

The excitement's all too much for the girls at a packed New Brighton pool. The Miss New Brighton Contest ended in 1989. After 40 years, today even the pool has gone.

Keith with 2 of the con testants in the early 6 Anyone know their name Yes it is Barry Farell in th backgroun

1959, the heyday of the bathing beauty contest. Legs waxed, hair coiffed, secure in their untouchable beauty, our leggy lovelies reveal how they love animals and children, and all want to be models and air hostesses.

No turning back now, Mammoth dismantles the floating part and dismantles the end.

It really was an impressive and grandoise pier.

Oh how great it all was. Is there no-one out there can bring the Glory back to New Brighton.

The Christmas Party can start as soon as the W.R.V.S. arrive with the false teeth.

This is New Brighton in Easter 1960, Busy, Brash and Mecca for the teenagers of the time. The Fair and Zoo were always crowded and there was so much to see.

Sept 1955 shows the Landing Stage at Birkenhead in tidy and well kept condition.

The Journey's nearly over but you can linger on the top deck, surrounded by the sights and sounds and smells of the Magic Mersey.

Poetry in Motion. As if in Silent Salute the Marine Lake pleasure craft reflect on the passing of a White Empress as the Empress of England 'slips out to sea' and an era draws to a close.

How I loved those afternoon walks in the Park with Dad,
when all we had to spend was time.